THE THIRTEEN SECRETS OF POETRY

To Maeve Binchy and Gordon Snell,
favourite writers and finest friends –
with love

*The compiler and publishers would like to thank the following for permission
to use copyright material in this collection:*

'I Remember Arnold' by John Lennon from *In His Own Write,* reprinted
by permission of Jonathan Cape; 'Spell to Banish a Pimple' by John
Agard from *Life Doesn't Frighten Me At All,* reprinted by permission of
William Heinemann Ltd; 'Double Glazing' by Brian Patten from
Gargling with Jelly, reprinted by permission of Viking Kestrel; 'At the
Marketplace' by Sujata Bhatt from *Brunizem,* reprinted by permission of
Carcanet Press Ltd; 'There Will Come Soft Rains' by Sara Teasdale from
Collected Poems, reprinted by permission of Macmillan Publishing Co;
'Rain' by Spike Milligan from *A Dustbin of Milligan,* reprinted by
permission of Viking Kestrel.

This collection first published in 1993 by
Simon & Schuster Young Books
Campus 400
Maylands Avenue
Hemel Hempstead
Herts HP2 7EZ

Reprinted in 1994

Printed and bound in Belgium by Proost International Book Production

British Library Cataloguing in Publication Data available

ISBN 0 7500 1379 6
ISBN 0 7500 1380 X (pb)

THE THIRTEEN SECRETS OF POETRY

Adrian Mitchell

Illustrated by Valerie Littlewood

SIMON & SCHUSTER
YOUNG BOOKS

Welcome to the Thirteen Secrets

* Five hundred years ago, when I was a baby, my father used to bounce me to the Scottish nursery rhyme 'Dance to Your Daddy'. Before I went to sleep my mother would read me poems that jumped and danced in my dreams. Soon I was making up my own rhymes – 'Molly and Polly, get your dolly', 'Gertie and Bertie, don't be dirty' – that sort of thing.

* I found that poems could be shouted, words could be chewed. Some words were frightening, some words were rude. Making poems was as much fun as making mud pies. (I loved to squeeze mud and smear it all over my hands as mud-gloves and over my face as a mud-mask and wait until it dried and cracked.)

* When I was fourteen I began to worry about questions like: What is love? Why do people kill each other? I started writing serious poems to explore these questions. Forty-five years later I'm still looking for the answers.

* I've always had lots of friends. But I find it hard to tell them what I feel inside my heart – except by writing poems. Poetry's a good way of talking or singing to your friends – and to complete strangers.

* Writing poems is fun and poems can be useful – but writing is also work. It takes time and imagination and skill. Skill? Yes. If you've ever built anything, from a sandcastle to a log cabin, you'll know that there an art to making – you don't just slap the sand or the wood together anyhow. Every art has its Secrets.

* So here are some of the Secrets of Poetry. I was going to tell you thirteen, but I've added eight extra to bring it up to twenty-one. The Secrets won't turn you into a Great Poet overnight. But they can help you to write all kinds of poems.

* Poetry is for everyone. Everybody has some poetry in them, just as everybody has a heart drumming away in their chest.

* Your heart beats before you're even born – and that's rhythm. You breathe in and out for as long as you live – and that's rhythm. A poem may have a regular rhythm like a heart beat. Or it may have a raggedy rhythm like the breathing of a puffed-out runner. But all poems need some kind of rhythm to keep them alive.

* There are all sorts of poems in the world. Some are very complicated and hard to understand. But a lot of the best poems are as clear and simple as a glass of water.

* So welcome to the Secrets. Remember – poetry can make you lots of friends, but it won't make you any money. If you'd rather have money than friends, don't write poetry.

SECRET ONE

Use your feet
to find the beat.

Walking down the street or across the playground, stomping on
earth or running on wet sand, let the rhythm of your feet act like a
drum-beat. The rhythm I chose for this wheelbarrow poem was
outright rock 'n' roll.

The Wildest Wheelbarrow

It's a Cadillac Subaru Bullnose Lada
With GBH overdrive
It's a Formula Zero
Robert de Niro
The most weed-unfriendly barrow alive
It's got rally-bred CD
Yes indeedy
With a floppy disc of solid steel
Yes it's the Wildest Wheelbarrow in the World
And it's riding on a wonky wheel

It's the Wildest Wheelbarrow in the World
I never saw another like that
So switch on the telly
And give it some welly
We'll be round the world in eighty seconds flat

It's a woodentop Jaguar Jumback Dolby
With hot and cold data base
It's stereo diesel
Runs like a weasel
With a spookerama smile upon its face
It's got a luxury fountain
A microfiche mountain
With a cotton-picking reel-to-reel
Yes it's the Wildest Wheelbarrow in the World
And it's riding on a wonky wheel

Adrian Mitchell

SECRET TWO

If the old word won't do
Make up a new.

Inventing new words is part of a poet's job. You'll find some in John Lennon's poem. You can also invent new names for places – Plumjam Park or Grombernark Alley – or for people (but they might name you back).

I Remember Arnold

I remember Kakky Hargreaves
As if 'twer Yestermorn'
Kakky, Kakky Hargreaves
Son of Mr Vaughan.

He used to be so grundie
On him little bike
Riding on a Sundie
Funny little tyke

Yes, I remember Kathy Hairbream
As if 'twer yesterday
Katthy, Kathy Hairbream
Son of Mr May

Arriving at the station
Always dead on time
For his destination
Now He's dead on line
(meaning he's been got by a train or something)

And so we growt and bumply
Till the end of time,
Humpty dumpty bumply
Son of Harry Lime.

    Bumbleydy Hubledy Humbley
    Bumdley Tum. (Thank you)

John Lennon

SECRET THREE

Don't write about Autumn
Because that's the season –
Write your poems
For a real reason.

LAUGH AND GROW FAT

LONG LIVE THE EARTH

NO MORE WAR

DOWN WITH PIMPLES

BONES

Some tribes make poems to bring down the rain or make the wheat grow tall. Some poets make poems to protest against starvation or to make a child laugh.

Spell to Banish a Pimple

Get back pimple
get back to where you belong

Get back to never-never land
and I hope you stay there long

Get back pimple
get back to where you belong

How dare you take up residence
in the middle of my face

I never offered you a place
beside my dimple

Get back pimple
get back to where you belong

Get packing pimple
I banish you to outer space

If only life was that simple

John Agard

SECRET FOUR

Write to cool down
Write to get hot
Write about things
You like a lot.

You can write down all your wishes in a poem. Maybe they'll come true and maybe not, but at least you'll have another poem.

The Lake Isle of Innisfree

I will arise and go now, and go to Innisfree,
And a small cabin build there, of clay and wattles made:
Nine bean-rows will I have there, a hive for the honey-bee,
And live alone in the bee-loud glade.

And I shall have some peace there, for peace comes dropping slow,
Dropping from the veils of the morning to where the cricket sings;
There midnight's all a glimmer, and noon a purple glow,
And evening full of the linnet's wings.

I will arise and go now, for always night and day
I hear lake water lapping with low sounds by the shore;
While I stand on the roadway, or on the pavements grey,
I hear it in the deep heart's core.

W B Yeats

SECRET FIVE

Write for other people;
Quite a few
Will sit down and write
A poem for you.

Poems make good extra birthday presents for people – your mum or dad or brother or sister or best friend. But it's also good to write poems that speak for people whose voices can't be heard – like Jenny in Brian Patten's poem.

Double Glazing

Jenny lives in a flat on the nineteenth floor
Of South McDougle Street.
Through the smudged-up double-glazed windows
The world looks calm and neat.

Jenny does not complain much
About the giant holes in her shoes.
She prefers to stare out of the window
And admire the distant views.

She'll not say nothing will Jenny,
About her pain and despair.
She's only a kid after all
And kids aren't supposed to care.

She'll not say nothing will Jenny,
She's a real tough nut to crack:
The kind of girl who always
Answers the teacher back.

Jenny lives in a flat on the nineteenth floor
Of South McDougle Street,
Through the smudged-up double-glazed windows
The world looks small and neat.

But down below it's crooked,
It is poor and full of hate,
And there are no double-glazed windows to stare through
When she's out and about the estate.

Brian Patten

SECRET SIX

Like a poppy-field poppy
Be happy to copy.

Tennyson was just starting to write poems when he made 'The Owl'. He borrowed the shape of the poem from a Shakespeare song. And why not? You should read every poet you can find and take all the help you can get.

The Owl

When cats run home and light is come,
And dew is cold upon the ground,
And the far-off stream is dumb,
And the whirring sail goes round,
And the whirring sail goes round;
Alone and warming his five wits,
The white owl in the belfry sits.

When merry milkmaids click the latch,
And rarely smells the new-mown hay,
And the cock hath sung beneath the thatch
Twice or thrice his roundelay,
Twice or thrice his roundelay;
Alone and warming his five wits,
The white owl in the belfry sits.

Alfred, Lord Tennyson

Secret Seven

Good ideas often fly off and so
Take that notebook wherever you go
(and three pens).

You may overhear a magical phrase on a bus, or find an amazing story in a newspaper or meet a dinosaur in the supermarket. Take out your notebook and scribble down what you see or hear or feel. Work on your scribbles later and some may turn into poems.

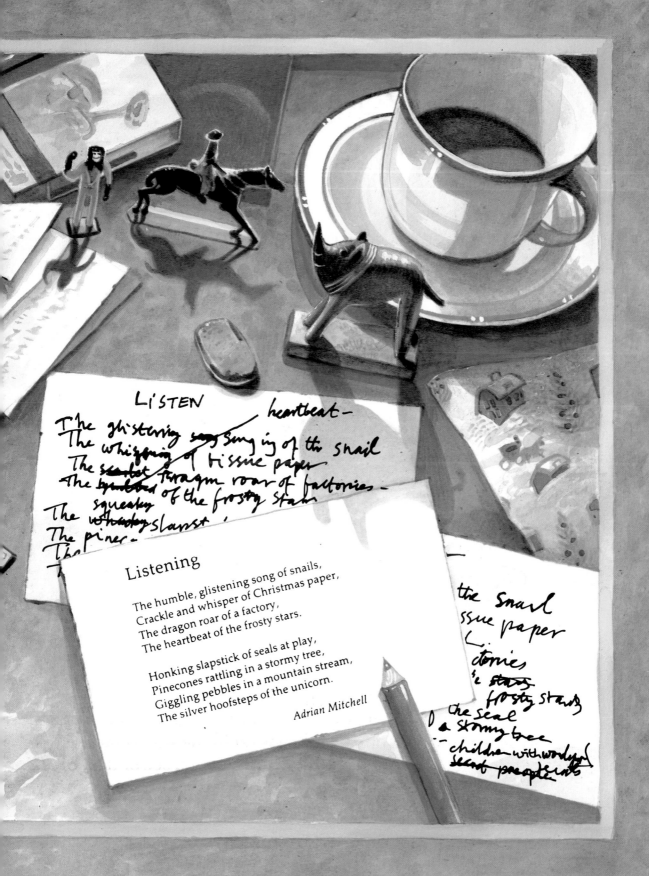

LISTEN

The glistening ~~song~~ Song ing of the snail   heartbeat—
The whispering of tissue paper.
The ~~scarlet~~ ~~dragon~~ dragon roar of factories—
The ~~symbol~~ squeaky of the frosty stars
The ~~whiskey~~ slapst '
The piner—
Th

Listening

The humble, glistening song of snails,
Crackle and whisper of Christmas paper,
The dragon roar of a factory,
The heartbeat of the frosty stars.

Honking slapstick of seals at play,
Pinecones rattling in a stormy tree,
Giggling pebbles in a mountain stream,
The silver hoofsteps of the unicorn.

Adrian Mitchell

the snail
issue paper
.
tories
e stars
frosty stars
the seal
a stormy tree
-- children with words
secret peacefuls

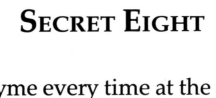

SECRET EIGHT

You can rhyme every time at the end of a line
And that's no crime if the words feel fine,
But on the other hand you can write a poem
Which doesn't have any rhymes at all.

Pleasant Sounds

The rustling of leaves under the feet in woods and under hedges;
The crumpling of cat-ice and snow down wood-rides, narrow lands,
    and every street causeway;
Rustling through a wood or rather rushing, while the wind hallows
    in the oak-top like thunder;
The rustle of birds' wings startled from their nests or flying unseen
    into the bushes;
The whizzing of larger birds overhead in a wood, such as crows,
    puddocks, buzzards;
The trample of robins and woodlarks on the brown leaves, and the
    patter of squirrels on the green moss;
The fall of an acorn on the ground, the pattering of nuts on the hazel
    branches as they fall from ripeness;
The flirt of the groundlark's wing from the stubbles – how sweet
    such pictures on dewy mornings, when the dew flashes from
    its brown feathers!

John Clare

SECRET NINE

What can you write about?
It helps very much
If you choose something
You can see and touch.

If you decide to write about a tree, look at that tree, touch it, smell it, climb it if you can. Write about what makes that tree different from all the other trees in the world. Same thing with people – but don't climb anyone shorter than you.

At the Marketplace

Look at the young jade-coloured artichokes!
Shall we have some for dinner?
Yes? No?
But wait. Look, there's fish in the next stall –
Oh to eat raw fish and raw onions and fresh
lemon juice and more raw fish –
juicy salt.
Eating raw fish
it doesn't matter if it's raining –
cold, and the umbrella
is blown aside – Eating raw fish
makes you feel like a mermaid through your legs –
Juicy salt.
I always crave sea salt, sour salt, strong eel salt.

Now there are purple sea horses all over her
and she is becoming a mermaid with artichoke skin.
Purple sea horses that he branded last night –
on her neck, shoulders, thighs: acrobatic purple,
elegant tattoo tails plunging deep into eel salt.
Sea horses are sucking on her salt
and she is talking like a mermaid, reasoning like a mermaid;
sea horses growing fuller and dark fat purple
and she eats another raw herring, swallowing
like a mermaid.

Sujata Bhatt

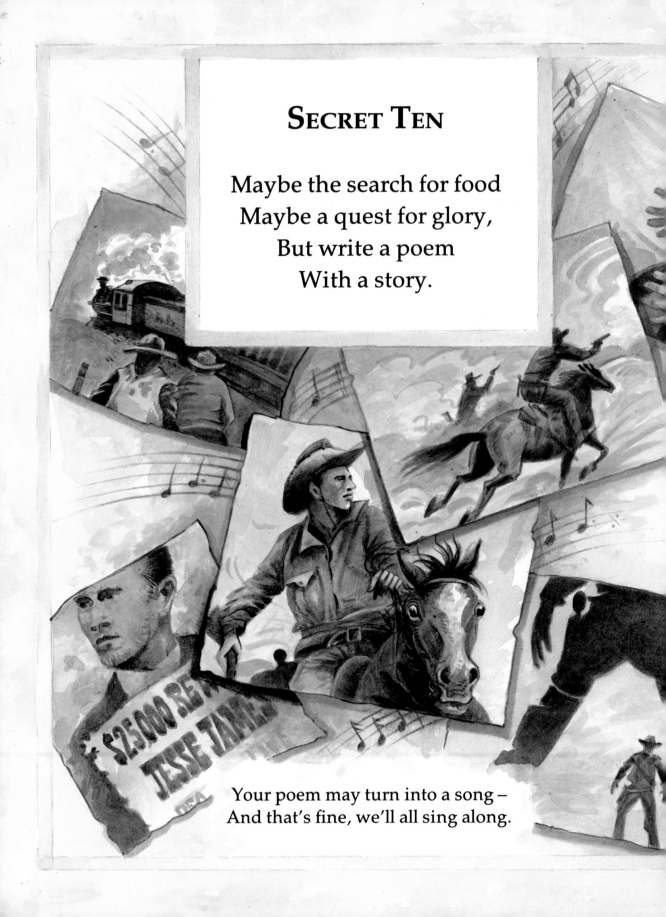

SECRET TEN

Maybe the search for food
Maybe a quest for glory,
But write a poem
With a story.

Your poem may turn into a song –
And that's fine, we'll all sing along.

Jesse James

*'Mister Howard' is the name Jesse James
used when he was hiding.

It was on a Wednesday night, the moon was shining bright,
    They robbed the Glendale train.
And the people they did say, for many miles away,
    'Twas the outlaws Frank and Jesse James.

Chorus – Jesse had a wife to mourn all her life,
        The children they are brave.
        'Twas a dirty little coward shot Mister Howard, *
        And laid Jesse James in his grave.

It was Robert Ford, the dirty little coward,
    I wonder how he does feel,
For he ate of Jesse's bread and he slept in Jesse's bed,
    Then he laid Jesse James in his grave. – *Chorus*

It was his brother Frank that robbed the Gallatin bank,
    And carried the money from the town.
It was in this very place that they had a little race,
    For they shot Captain Sheets to the ground. – *Chorus*

They went to the crossing not very far from there,
    And there they did the same;
And the agent on his knees he delivered up the keys
    To the outlaws Frank and Jesse James. – *Chorus*

It was on a Saturday night, Jesse was at home
    Talking to his family brave,
When the thief and the coward, little Robert Ford,
    Laid Jesse James in his grave. – *Chorus*

How people held their breath when they heard of Jesse's death,
And wondered how he ever came to die.
'Twas one of the gang, dirty Robert Ford,
That shot Jesse James on the sly. – *Chorus*

Anon

SECRET ELEVEN

Pile up your feelings
On a poetry plate –
Write about something
You really hate.

homework BULLIES WAR pimples sneering

GRISTLE MAGGOTS

toothache School dinners DRUM MACHINES February

Sara Teasdale hated war, but only because she loved people.
So when she wrote about the cruelty and horror of war,
she made a very gentle poem.

There Will Come Soft Rains

There will come soft rains and the smell of the ground,
And swallows circling with their shimmering sound;

And frogs in the pools singing at night,
And wild plum-trees in tremulous white.

Robins will wear their feathery fire
Whistling their whims on a low fence-wire;

And not one will know of the war, not one
Will care at last when it is done.

Not one would mind, neither bird nor tree,
If mankind perished utterly;

And Spring herself, when she woke at dawn
Would scarcely know that we were gone.

Sara Teasdale

SECRET TWELVE

To make a poem
That lasts a minute
Daydream for hours
Before you begin it.

Daydreaming is like going to the movies in your head – but you're in charge of the camera and the story. Try to see the pictures as clearly as you can. If you can't find words for those pictures, try painting them instead or turning them into music.

The Wind Has Such a Rainy Sound

The wind has such a rainy sound
   Moaning through the town,
The sea has such a windy sound, –
   Will the ships go down?

The apples in the orchard
   Tumble from their tree. –
Oh will the ships go down, go down,
   In the windy sea?

Christina Rossetti

Rain

There are holes in the sky
   Where the rain gets in,
But they're ever so small
   That's why rain is thin.

Spike Milligan

SECRET THIRTEEN

Don't just write
For the literate few –
Write for babies
And animals too.

Poem to be Said to a Dog
While Tickling her Chest

Good dog
Good Polly
Good dog
Good Polly

Adrian Mitchell

Poem to be Played with a Baby

Ring the bell – ding ding! *(Pull the baby's ear – gently.)*

Press the buzzer – bzzzzz! *(Press the baby's nose.)*

Knock at the door – knock knock! *(Knock on its forehead.)*

And walk in – Oh no, thank you! *(Put your little finger in the
baby's mouth. Pretend that the baby
has bitten you.)*

*(Note: Only try this on a baby you know. You should wash your hands first.
Demonstrate the poem on your own ear, nose, forehead and mouth several times before you try it on
the baby. After a few performances, the baby should laugh after it tries to bite you. When they get the
joke, babies find this poem very funny. Health warning: Some babies have Count Dracula pointy teeth
and will bite you properly. Read them some other poem.)*

Adrian Mitchell

Extra Secrets

14. When you read to a friend
    Or recite to a crowd
    Say your poem
    Slow and loud.

15. Poetry's a lovely, dangerous game
    But it's very unlikely to bring you fame
    And don't try to live by your poetry
    You'd earn more selling cat food on Mercury.

16. Sad poems, funny poems –
    Feel everything you're writing.
    Rough poems, gentle poems –
    Make them all – exciting.

17. It's pretty tiring
    Just being you –
    Write from other people's
    Point of view.
    Use lots of voices and you may
    End up with a poem
    That becomes a play.

18. All you can do with your life
    Is live it.
    Poetry's a gift –
    So give it.

19. If you want to learn
    How to talk to grass
    Or dance the giraffe
    Or imitate glass
    Invite a poet
    Into your class.

20. Write a secret poem
    That you never show.
    Learn it and burn it
    So nobody will know.

21. These are secrets.
    None of them are rules.
    Here's another secret:
    There are no rules in poetry.
    (Except the ones you make
    up for yourself.)

What to do When You Find a Poem You Like

Read it again
And write it
Learn it by heart
Recite it
Sing it
Rave it
Paint it on a flag
And wave it

Feed it
Ride it
Climb right down
Inside it
Fly on its back
For a night and a day
Then pat it and kiss it
And give it away

Goodbye and good luck with the secrets!